W9-BQR-789

17517

For Babs
with love
Mary —

September 25, 1970

RIDE INTO MORNING

RIDE INTO MORNING

POEMS

by

MARY KENNEDY

Gotham Book Mart
New York
1969

Grateful acknowledgment is made to the Editors of the publications in which certain of these poems first appeared.

Meadow: American Scholar © 1968
The Unfortunate Mole: Voice in the Night,
One of the Sidhe: Saturday Review © 1953, © 1954
A Wreath of Four O'clocks: Good Housekeeping © 1959
Venus and the Polar Bear: McCall's © 1964

Other poems are reprinted by the courtesy of the following magazines: Harper's Bazaar, The Ladies Home Journal, Voices, New York Herald Tribune, Imprints Quarterly, American Weave, Variegations, The Lyric, Botteghe Oscure.

Monogram designed by Deems Taylor.

Copyright © Mary Kennedy, 1969

Library of Congress Catalog Card Number 75-95240

PRINTED IN THE UNITED STATES OF AMERICA

For those I love
among the living
and among the dead

CONTENTS

RIDE INTO MORNING

COME AWAY

THE SUDDEN DAY

WE SHARE THE WORLD

CON DOLORE

RIDE INTO MORNING

MEADOW

The moon piercing through apple leaves
struck me. I turned in my bed
and eyed the shadows. The stars
unmoving, moved, retreating,
faded against sudden brightness . . .
so brilliant is a moon on the wane.
The night held back something.
There was more to come. . . .
It might be that I had a part in it.
I swung my feet out of bed
and roused the sleeping grasses.

WARBLERS

Sycamore, singing beside the path
Pied brown and yellow-green:
Minstrel in medieval wool
Made half of shadow;
No leaves, but confident of growth,
I hear your song.

In the summer orchard
Small birds the color of new apples,
Color of yellow green apples
Cling to the fruit,
Hide behind the leaves
Fluttering and squeaking,
Then rush with careless song
And light-struck feathers
Into the sky.

And we, already inhabitants
Of Paradise . . . no less than they,
Hear Caedmon's angel calling,
"Sing me something!"
And move about in the mystery of green
Filled with immeasurable joy.

RIDE INTO MORNING

It is my young mother driving along
the sandy roads of my childhood,
and there am I, a child of four,
sitting proudly beside a lovely lady.
On the way, on the way, on the way somewhere!
Swiftly moving into a beckoning unknown.
The horse is called Barney
after a friend of my father's.
A happy neigh as he answers the rein's urging,
with high-stepping, proud prancing,
brown haunches rocking, tail swishing
over the buckboard. His hooves
leave round marks in the damp white sand.
The wheels of the buggy splash as we ford
the leaf-brown waters of a shallow creek.
Morning coolness touches my face.
The air is sharp with pine.
A small tortoise in the road:
My mother reins in old Barney
and waits for it to cross...a round
dark object with thrusting eager head.
In its own time. In its own time.
I lean my cheek against the white muslin
of her sleeve. Contentedly I sense
that I, too, shall not be hurried.

Mother, turn! Look deeply into my eyes,
Reveal yourself. When I am an old woman
I shall long to understand, to know you
as you are now. To be sure that you know
of the love spilling over, as I sit trustfully
beside you, riding into the silver morning.
I hear the hoof beats, as my mother and I
and the times we lived in,
go softly thudding into oblivion.

MORE PRECIOUS THAN GRASS

More precious than grass
Is the white sand under the palm trees.
Closer to my heart than grey
Northern oceans
Is the blue of the Bay, the blue
Of the quiet waters of the southern seas.
These things I knew as a child
And I left them
For other places more valued by many:
Yet never found again the peace
I had forsaken,
Nor the child that I had been.

A WREATH OF FOUR O'CLOCKS

The wreaths of four o'clocks, silken red,
we wove as children,
ruffled leis of fluted edges. . . .
I wish I had one now
to fling over your head,
to give you as a token.

The long afternoon was spent
in laborious delight,
ignoring the inquisitive buzzing
of an occasional bee,
sinking into a comfortable emptiness
beyond sound:
the pointed blossoms in bright heaps
beside us on the grass,
or precise in rows
upon the patterned bricks of the walk.
We endured the moving sun,
the furry scent of the coarse lantana,
until we looked into the rose of sunset . . .
the clouds curling like petals
and even the air dyed pink.

For all the love I've never spoken,
take this offering.
The child who made it,
threading the pierced flowers
on a dark thread,
thinking it wonderful to make a pretty thing . . .
that child is here behind the mask I wear.
She loved you then, not knowing love,
and loves you now
aware of all it means.

REACHING FOR ANGELS

They come in troops
when summoned,
angels in every color,
steady of purpose.
Invisible mostly,
although I have seen them,
one angel, or twenty
superior beings
accomplishing impossible
tasks in a breath,
in the time of a merry
ringing of a bell.
My life in their hands,
my burden lifted
and the angel has flown
or the bright troop
has scattered:
but they are within call.
With the speed of light
they will come again
when we cry in anguish
or terror
or desperate need . . .
leaving their wings
hung on a cloud,
sleeves rolled up for work,
disguised
as earthly creatures,
but not hiding
their compassionate eyes.

THE QUEEN'S SWANS

The Queen's white swans
full of light and longing
fly over the palace gardens.
What intricacies of time
sculptured this icy grace,
this passionate restraint of line,
this wonder?

Does the Queen look up and see them
proud and strong and shining . . . ?
Does she say:
Those are my swans, wild and free,
they belong to the Crown,
they belong to the Queen,
they belong to me!

There are my intrepid swans
flying for me.

All the wild swans in England
belong to the Queen.
I know what I know;
where they go I, too, shall go;
where they have been
I also have been,
there shall I be.

I sit with the Council
serenely replying,
but the spirit blows as it wills
with a song as it goes,
and over far lands and wild seas
the swans are flying.

THE TRIBUTE BEARERS

The dust is deep
On the golden bowl
The rust upon the sword.
Time rots the threads of tribute silk
And sable feeds the moth.

Brown for the Sung,
Green for the Ming,
Pale yellow for the powerful Ch'ing.
But the brown has passed,
The green retreated,
And on the dragon the yellow is seated.

Over the mountains through mists or snow
While Embassies cross the plains below,
From every side, on every hand
Struggling through sleet or blowing sand,
Reeking jungles, roaring rivers,
They carry the world's treasure
For the Son of Heaven's pleasure.
Bales of tissue and painted silk,
Lacquer and fur and falcon's feathers,
And wild ginseng for potency
And promise of immortality.

Down from the black north,
From blue valleys in the east,
From the warm red south,
The colorless west,
From Ki Chou, Yen Chou, and the valleys of Tai,
The tribute bearers bring the tax
To lay at his feet, implore his grace.

Kuan-yin, where are your merciful eyes?

Great bells ringing along the way,
Elephant, donkey and camel train,
But man is the overburdened beast
Who bears the load no beast could bear
And peers like a beast from his tangled hair.

Bent low in dust is straining man.
Nothing between him and the scorching sun
But the lotus leaf he holds on high,
Snatched in passing from lapping pond,
A fragile shade for an aching eye.

On perilous, freezing mountain paths
So little warmth in a padded coat
That many a lad is left there dead,
Adding his load to another's back.
Losing nothing along the way,
For even a carven olive pit
May bring a smile to majestic lips.
Vats of varnish, iron ingots,
Blocks of marble, peachbloom vases,
And cages of jeweled singing birds
That on the hour chant their songs
While fountains of bright glass and light
Minute by minute tell the night
And trees of jade cast opulent shade.

What silken hangings fall between
The august eyes and the toiling men
Who sweat and starve while a golden hoard
Mounts to ceilings and fills the rooms
Of latticed houses that row on row
Rim a forbidden city?

What stuff? I say.
Ah, here's a shred of greenish yellow,
Of rarest silk that lines the way,
The imperial mile the Emperor rides
When he goes to the feast of spring.

Straight to the temple, then back again,
A furrow ploughed . . . his lesson to men . . .
While all the way is hung with silk
To shut from his sight the poor and old
The leper, the hungry, the blind, the cold.

Sheltered by rustling silken walls,
He cannot see where misery lives:
Lord of the many-colored lands
Purple and yellow, brown and green
And the white mohammedan sands.

Does the Emperor bear a mind distressed,
A weary head to the pillow pressed,
A heavy heart, a lonely soul
And nowhere to turn for an answering eye?
He climbs to wonder when nights are long,
Over the strange wave-eaten rocks
That were brought to him from the Yellow Sea,
What it is like outside the walls.
His life but a leaf on the tree of life. . . .
How find the tree?
How fathom the thought beyond the show?

Ho Shen deceived him, but that was past.
Weary and aging he leaves at last
And gives his throne to his son to lose,
His rhinoceros cup and his jeweled shoes.
Gives them all and with heavy looks
Goes into his study, to his books.

He does not know that the day will come
When no one will sit on the peacock throne;
When pointed hands will spill the pearls
That were proof against fire
And charm against flood,
That jade and ruby will furnish thieves;
The exquisite faces fade away

Wreathed in artemisia leaves. . . .
The obsequious vanish, with all their bowing,
Crouched on the pavements abased in fear:
And the cruel magnificence, blazing pride
That grasped the world in a dragon's claw,
Will end in tears, and a net of terror,
Will end in a brain-washed man
In a worker's denim of faded blue.*

Brown for the Sung,
Green for the Ming,
Pale yellow for the powerful Ch'ing.

The lizards run on the palace tiles,
Grass uproots the marble walks,
And emptiness stretches miles on miles.

> *The dust is deep*
> *On the golden bowl.*
> *The rust upon the sword.*
> *Time rots the threads of tribute silk*
> *And sable feeds the moth.*

---

*Time Magazine, October 27, 1967, records the death, at age sixty-one, of P'u Yi, the last Emperor of China. Crowned at the age of two, deposed at the age of six, after many vicissitudes, he was allowed by the Communists to spend the last years of his life working in the gardens of Peking.

OBLIQUE REVENGE

Out of airy green
old worm
you wove this silk

yet someone else
has profited
by your urge

toward flying.
Is the dream
all that we leave?

I continue to weave
Forgetting dying.

COME AWAY

(

COME AWAY

Come out of the jungle, Lydia, the mud is deep.
The roots of trees and ferns and grasses are asleep,
Why talk to them?
The wind does not blow, the leaves hang tangled and still.
Fragile birds shake and shiver beside the muddy river.
Over velvet stones, vines twist, slither and slide,
Bright-eyed in the shadows enormous creatures hide.
A ripple of fur in green flickering light. . . .
Is there a prowling leopard with the soft name of Lydia?
Lydia, Lydia, come away, come away.
Monkeys swing high in the white trees.
Nearer creeps the furtive baboon.
Roots glide, the rock comes alive.
Run, Lydia, run.
Slip silently past the flamingoes,
Stretching their scarlet wings, winding their long necks
In the hot lagoon.
Reticent and proud the troubled lion passes.
Take care! Take care! Come away.
Roll out of the relentless mud.
Stretch on the deep soft moss and run.
Come out of the jungle.
Lydia. Lydia.

INTERLUNAR

Gazing into the pool,
they saw themselves reflected,
not as they thought they were,
not even as they wished to be . . .
but gathering green shadows
gave back curious faces
with eyes aslant and mouths
austere and full of question.

THE WOODS AT TWILIGHT

In the green gloom I seem to walk undersea:
pale green starfish cling to the hemlocks,
underfoot, tiny darting creatures in the bog.
Overhead, tossed by invisible tides,
whirling with fishlike motion,
the trembling bat.

Speak, all you beings of twilight!
Green frog,
moths caught by the swaying reeds,
purple-robed, or flitting moon pale in the murky light.
Lucent water lilies floating
on the black gleaming pond.

> A whisper, a moan,
> a shimmer of sound in the dark,
> the crying of leaves. . . .

A presence gathers near me in the air,
leaping along a gust of wind,
spiraling upward into a boundless element.
Then a flood of silence.

Something fled the wood because I came.

ONE OF THE SIDHE

Let her rest,
Winged wild thing
Blown on the storm.
Do not fear
Her wide sad eyes,
Her lightning glances.
Have you never heard
Of a creature lost in air
Drawn by a flame?
Watch!
She moves to the fire,
Grateful, meek.
Blow on her fingers
Frozen with cold.
If you are gentle
Perhaps she will speak;
If you are kind
She may forget sorrow.
Let her rest now,
She will be gone tomorrow.
When morning comes
She will fade into mist.
Only for this night
Has she need of shelter.
Guard your heart well.
She will try to surprise,
To bewitch, to bind,
To take it with a spell
With an ember and an ash,
For she could be cured
By its strength
Of all she has endured.
Pity will not hold her:
Only love could change her
Into simple woman.

You are not in danger
If she leaves unkissed.

Green in her eyes,
Bronze in her hair:
Do you see the flash
Of fool's fire there?
It is such a light
As lures a man to doom . . .
But you are safe, my darling,
In your little room.

MIDSUMMER IN NEW FOREST

Behind the heavy beeches
I saw it move
Through the smoky
Translucence of leaves,
A thin pale red,
A jagged white.
So swift it sped
Scarcely stirred
The faint hazy green
In the nebulous light.

For an instant
I had stared into eyes
Mesmeric and sensuous,
A king in a cloak
Of summer,
A king of faery
As well I knew.
An arrogant look
And he had gone
Although I called
His name
Through corridors
Of green:
Oberon!
He would not turn.
Around me echoed
Whispered voices,
None my own,
Oberon! Oberon!

LILIES

"No lilies on Wednesday," she said,
Already I have forgotten why,
For I seemed to see all the fields of Bermuda
with their smooth buds tight shut,
and all the waxen lilies in the gardens
of New England
withdrawn under green leaves.
"Wednesday," mourned the wind, "alas, alas,
no lilies . . . no lilies, shall I tell you why?"
Wind and echo murmured, "Why? . . . why?"

Then in a dream I saw the wedding day,
with damsels all in white,
and lilies shorn from my own garden
heaped along their arms;
with medieval faces full of question,
and woeful eyes downcast.
Then would they move away, and come again
without the lilies,
but each one held a lighted lamp,
that shone upon her garments falteringly.
Slowly as ripples might refresh a stream,
with solemn grace, almost as if they danced,
one and then another, bent, blew out a flame.

Yet when I waked, I did not understand.

ANTIQUE DILEMMA

She's there!
Flying from the casement in a shadowy dress,
Every ribbon waving.

Yet here she is, discreet as a primrose,
Decked in a fichu, gazing on the garden.
Only her head, it's true, but seeming very steady,
Made of a marble as smooth as living flesh.
One wonders what the sculptor knew
When he carved the features,
Stone head, untroubled by a weedy garden,
An encroaching sea, a ruined castle,
Huge and empty.

Why is she jumping from a gaping window
Out of the ivy, smiling and expectant,
Dressed for a journey?

Gravely the antique head looks on old flower beds,
Stares past the bronze sphinx half hidden among ilex,
Not seeing the ecstatic wraith
Of a girl, four centuries in earth,
Leaping to meet a lover who is no longer there.

Then she is not in the garden,
For the head is stone,
And long gone is the moment that set its seal on air.
Serene, unreflective head,
Ghost with no heart, no breath, no tears. . . .
Yet something of her lingers
In a searching wing, a fragrance,
While the towers crumble,
And the green grows wild.

The stone head stares at ruin.
The apparition smiles.

Owls cry in the roofless hall,
Persistent waves beat upon black rocks
Whispering beneath the cliff,
"We have come to the end of our time."

Alone.
In a desolate place.
Even I was not there.

GAME

Children playing *statues*
hear in deep memory
the old command of "stop!"
and whirl from a companion's hand
to self-analysis.

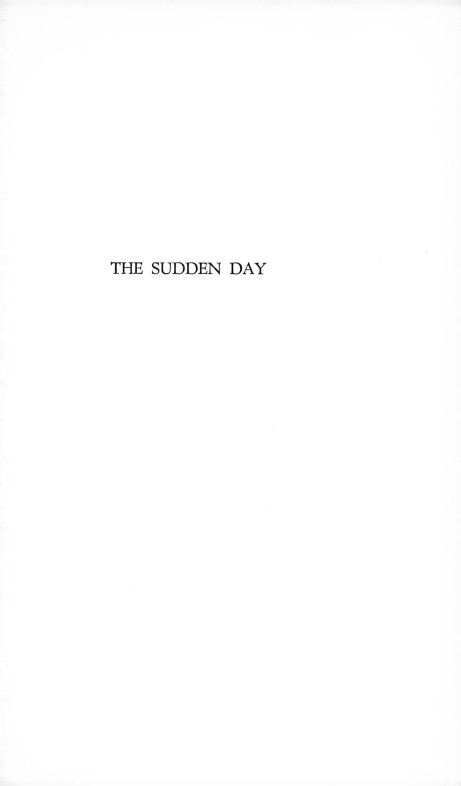

THE SUDDEN DAY

THE SUDDEN DAY

How did it come to be summer?
The poppies full-blown,
The birds full-voiced.
Where could I have been
While this day was preparing?
The inchworm does not answer,
The little green inchworm
Tickling my hand,
Measuring me for my shroud.

THE INDOLENT GARDENER

Jungle
      takes over the garden.
Day after day creepers weave impenetrable walls.
Flowers have gone wild, making a woven defense
    against intruders,
their strong roots intertwined, to trip, to overthrow.
Jewel weed grows tall and thick.
Great branches lie where they have fallen;
the tree uprooted blocks the paths, blotting out the sky.
On sunniest days scars of hurricane are on this land.

Some morning
      monkeys will come trooping and chattering.
Tigers will slink through the forest of phlox,
rutile deer romp and leap through the mock-orange,
panthers drop from tree limbs that grasp and tangle
    over the pool:
From quince and pear and wild willow,
out of grape leaves grasping the top of the elm,
panthers will drop.
Elephants will push through the sagging pergola,
a bird of paradise alight on the blighted maple,
while peach-colored parakeets sit in innocent pairs
on the stone wall among the euonymus.
When night falls, mouse-like nocturnal creatures
will come out of the heaving ground to scamper
    in the moonlight.

Then
      will the bulbul sing its enchanting song . . .
until we forget vanished larkspur and madonna lilies,
and the civilized scent of herbs.

A CLEAR TITLE

Come out, come out:
You bought the night with the house.
The moon goes with it
And that clear green star.
The constellations are yours, too,
The light-struck clouds.
Morning was included.
The deed gave you the migratory birds,
The woodpecker and warbler,
The crested cardinal
Rushing across the spring
With such a show of feathers.
Do not cower inside four walls,
You have bought the Universe.

ARCANE

This is my speech, my language,
    this clear bird-song with rippled notes beneath . . .
    these birds, my kinsmen, once my pensioners.
For punctuation of their message,
    . . . this sublime advice, so delicately spoken-sung, . . .
I have the very sun, the moving shadows
    of the pointed leaves, the purple tree trunks,
    the smooth cut hill.
I share the mysteries they know,
    for I have learned this syntax
    through solitary years;
And when each cadence falls or fills,
    or when inflection means some other thing,
    it stirs the heart's long listening.
There is no gainsaying
    the period of a sudden wing.

THE BEST BUTTER

Butter
buried in the peat bog
of ancient Ireland
though not edible
is still visible,
is yellow and hard,
in tall leather vessels,
churn-shaped,
ragged and blackened
by the sleeping years.

Do we learn
that much which is saved
is useless
even if it keeps
an outward seeming?
Do we learn
that while we are living
we should eat up our butter?
Or do scientists remark
on the preservative
characteristics of peat?
This frugal quality
in our ancestors,
hitherto unsuspected,
tells us that Cuchulain
and the heroes . . .
or perhaps it was Emer
and the matchless ladies . . .
used the bog
as a refrigerator.

I am really at a loss
as to how to study
this lesson.

Was it some reluctance
for housekeeping that caused
Emer to forget the butter
while she sang wild songs
and wandered
on the low, green hills?
The songs have come down to us,
and hills and songs
are still usable.

HOLDING A BOOK OF WORDS

I hold it in my hand,
Nothing but words,
The raw stuff of poems.
I feel as Madame Curie may have felt
Before those tons of pitchblende.
Is there radium there
And can I find it?
How many years of sorting, searching,
Shoveling, before the few
Precious grains lie
In the small vessel of my life
And illumine the darkness?

GARDEN UNDER SNOW

Seen once before, but only in a dream
A vision of bronzes heaped with snow.
Into this enchantment comes
One I love, moving in reverie
Among the dark dignities of laurel and fir:
Where framed in drifted white
The ice in the pool
Takes on a nameless color:
Where plane trees in motley
Have the look of a distant land
Along decorous flagstones.
Into this ageless garden,
Far away in the country of the mind,
He comes, with light upon his meditative face,
And we meet after the long parting,
Among bronzes blurred with snow,
In air of glass.

THIS PRECIOUS LIGHT

Idly we see
that columbine is blooming,
pink buds of clover thrusting
through the grass, yet hear no echo
of solemn days entombing love
nor know the flowers withering
as we pass.
This is the summer, anodyne and rune,
sending white roses under
a rose-white moon, while transitory
vines try to trap the stars.
It will all be over
and no word of truth be spoken.
Through the color and the dazzle
we cannot see an ending. . . .
But one of us is captured
with things that are departing.
As violets vanish the larkspur
is starting. My darling, my darling,
the dark and cold are coming!

CORAL REEF

Where in time past
        the ending to our love?
I cannot find the mark
        that fell upon that instant.
Yet barring all return
        an invisible wall
        begun by something small,
As coral forms
        impenetrably hard,
        unscalable in height,
Beneath calm waters
        in the Melanesian sea,
So we
        have made and must endure
This separation.

THE EARTH MOVES

Now in a mist of green, the turning year
befuddles, entices:
throwing a veil over reality,
clothing skeleton boughs in freshness,
making a new thing of old Earth,
urging the heart to take on illusion.

> The Earth moves.
> It is the mole awakening.
> Roots stretch, thrust. Buds swell, burst . . .
> first the peach, then the pear,
> then the deep pink of the sheep-nose apple.
> The bulb releases the daffodil.
> The squill dances across the grass,
> blue as Egypt.

What can release the desperate mind?
Lacking love, yet lost in love,
intolerable loneliness,
the indignity of supplication.

So we talk of the weather, the weather.
We hide defeat under cliché and laughter,
"April so rainy!"

> The dark cedars are slantwise
> with the effort of resisting snow and ice.
> They have not slept.
> We are the earth-bound, the lonely,
> learning to lean with the wind.

SONG OF THE COLD

Cut back the roses,
Winter is upon us,
All the old bloom
Is withered and brown,
Cut them down.
From the roots
Will come new shoots
And other roses,
But the ones I grew
Have perished;
And he is gone
Whom most I cherished.
Cut back the roses,
Winter has come.

WE SHARE THE WORLD

ESCAPE INTO SMALLNESS

Fling yourself eye level with the grass.
Look at the aphis toiling
through a forest of moss.
Life, lifting a ponderous wave,
breaks into small forms,
amusing, exquisite, ridiculous. . . .
They are the laughter of Creation,
drops splashed from its thundering breakers.

Insects bending in the middle,
carelessly hinged on a thread,
praying mantis, greedy hypocrite,
the bee, fat and heavy, a Croesus
carrying his money bags strapped to his legs;
the butterfly, all silk and powder,
enameled ladybug, ecstatic glowworm,
dark wasp,
the indefatigable, regimented ant,
a stick that walks,
button-eyed darning needle stitching the air.
Each humming its own weird tune
in the symphony of summer.

The insect escapes from the moss.
In such a merry world
Who dares prolong his grief?

THE UNFORTUNATE MOLE

In the night the agile mole
Seeking for a water hole
Behind his sensitive pale hands,
Skillfully advancing,
With his pointed scholar's nose
Curling eager for a drink
And his monkey fashioned toes
Pushing him too near the brink.
Reckless, swift, his spirits lift.
Quivering in his sightless face
As he nears the cool wet place.
Small and soft and trusting
From the hard earth thrusting,
Poor blind mole to tumble down,
To fall so far and then to drown.
Drowned, alas! in a midnight minute,
Reaching the pool he fell right in it:

Who now on the yielding surface lies.
Earth-conscious face turned to the skies,
Soft fur and fine, disheveled, wet,
His gentlemanly hands astonished yet.
The long meek fingers elegantly spread
Protest the indignity of being dead.

Mourn an instant this mechanism wasted
With so much of his small life untasted.
He was grey, slender, quick, clever,
Neatly, excellently put together.

He knew the feel of friable earth,
He could test for clay,
For dirt or gravel,
Could make a road on which to travel.
He knew the nature of rock and stone,
And dark days and nights endured alone,

He could nibble roots,
And gather fruits.
And provide for the future of son and daughter,
But little or nothing he knew of water.

Alas!
The unfortunate mole!

THE LIZARD

There's a leaf-green lizard in the vine,
Pale as spring and sudden as a squall.
Jewel-eyed dragon, reduced in scale,
He threaded a swift, thin tail over the limb
Where moon flowers weigh upon the pine.
As scared as I, he scrambled up the wall
Then tumbled on the hedge
Trembling into stone, changing from bright to dim.
Little things are everywhere in danger,
Are quiet at a shadow,
Half disappear before a sound.
Withdraw, stay hid beneath the anger,
Wish to be anywhere but where they are:
Near things but partly seen
Lose their triumphant green.

ABOUT YOUR MOUSE

I saw your mouse,
An inch of feathery fur
in hunched quiet
nibbling;
soft, clean, new;
poised on a stepping-stone
near tufts of mint
outside my door;
so young, not yet afraid;
eyes bright with light
on a dark surface,
tiny feet
slim and white;
tail
longer than mouse,
and pale;
half its length a head
triangular with chin,
and on the upper corners
transparent ears
tucked in.
It felt my shade
without alarm,
abandoned nibbling,
hopped away,
then stopped to play
sliding on an apple.
O, Master Craftsman,
I love your mouse . . .
even when I hear him
gnawing at the doorsill
scrabbling in the wall. . . .
Love once given
is beyond recall.

VENUS AND THE POLAR BEAR

Stretching soft paws, he waked, the pale, sad bear.
Twisting within his dreams, a thrust of pain
Roused him at dawn to walk his cage again.
Angry that narrow head, those eyes, golden, deep,
As he swung fiercely in a rhythm half of sleep.
Then rose Venus, shining widely, shining whitely,
Gleaming through the captive air.
She had been there, those many years ago,
When sovereign over the unvarying snow,
The timeless reach of Arctic was their field
And not an inch would either of them yield
Of solitude, so much they both loved space
To stretch in, both the planet and he.
As he outpaced his violent misery,
She, sparkling, called him by his Arctic name.
Nanuk he was, the feared, the formidable.
Then he took heart, unmindful of his shame,
For into limitless sky she beckoned brightly. . . .
A sky twice-wide, as were the frozen lands
Where he swam in crystal currents nightly
Or prowled among the moving hills of ice.
In the clutching prison of the city park,
He stood companioned in the luminous dark.

WHOM THE GODS LOVE DIE YOUNG

Tread warily, speak softly, old woman,
Adders lurk on this path.
Do not remind anyone that you are here.
Move along, but quietly.
You have loved them. . . . It is nothing.
You have given for a lifetime
The work of your hands. They think
There will always be love and giving.
You are in the way now
And their anger could rend you.
Do not speak unless spoken to,
And when you answer speak carefully.
You have done nothing wrong
But you are still here.

It is that which angers them.

LEGEND

When Bede was old and stricken blind,
with most of his great work done . . .
a long-lost disciple in bitter jest,
one rainy day, came whispering,
"A multitude in silence stands
upon the hill hoping to hear your word."
Bede put on finely woven, brocaded vesture,
and stumbled darkly up the rough steep path,
where on the barren height
waited only the wind,
waited a heap of stones.
Lifting his sightless eyes
he spoke his thoughts
with all the fervor of a generous heart,
then raised his hands to bless the emptiness
before him, his old face luminous.
"Forever and ever," he prayed.
The stones replied, "Amen, O Venerable Priest,
Amen, Amen," cried the stones.
Cried the stones.

SALOME

At first I said
I could not cause a man to die,
I would not ask his head.

But it was terrible to see her face.
He had insulted her, the Queen, she cried.
We would be driven out, unless John died.

She taught me how I must dance.
In a frenzy of longing, she said.
"More than that, Salome," she kept insisting,
"More, more, bend to the floor . . . rise up, rise up,
Stretch like a cat . . . running, turning, twisting . . .
Now again, like that . . . Salome!

"But take each veil off slowly, slowly, your eyes up,
And the last veil do not take off at all,
Let it slip a little way from the shoulder
And breast, as though you might let it fall
In another instant. Look at the King!"

I remembered all she had said,
I felt like the madwoman who shouts along the way.
Wild as a tiger, . . . cruel, gentle. . . . I rode on wings
        of air. . . .
And at the last I wished I were a child, and then I stopped.
I held the veil around me before I let it drop.
I could see the King was pleased.

Ask! Salome, ask!

"The head of the Baptist," I said,
"The man in prison . . . give me his head."
I fell at the King's feet and clutched his knee.
"Bring her cloak," he said, and someone covered me.

We waited while they led him to the block.
I wanted to cry, "Oh, no, oh, no, O King,
Do not give me this bloody thing!"
But I saw the hatred in my mother's eyes
And I was silent. Lying against his robes, I stayed there,
exhausted by the dance; his hand entangled in my hair.

They brought the head on a silver charger.
When I saw it, my knees broke under me. I could not stand.
Someone held me . . . the King, perhaps, reached me
        his hand.

I saw the beauty of the thin face, the vigilant jaw,
The gentle mouth that had spoken only truth,
The calmness of the brow.
There was a light within that lit the face.
This dead was living, more than those who are living now.

Something left me then, my heart, my hope,
My life itself. O holy man from the river Jordan,
Beautiful young man, I take your pain.
John, John, your pardon, pardon! I shall not dance again!

IN SEARCH OF THOREAU AND EMERSON

How did we come to Concord
and beyond to the pile of stones,
the cairn at Walden?
The way led through Lexington, Lincoln,
we passed Waltham, Watertown, Cambridge,
skirted Sudbury Marsh:
through juniper on the hillsides,
pine along the roadways,
shadberry and barberry bright in widening valleys.

There is peace at Walden
a sharp, sweet scent of pine,
a lake, round as a moonstone.
I thought how a man had lived alone
in those woods during all the seasons.
Working and writing through the quick spring,
the unhurrying summer,
hewing wood; "making the earth say beans
instead of weeds," until autumn blazed
through the woven leaves, calling him
to contemplation as the fires died.
He endured the ghostlike stillness of winter,
breathless in severe cloisters of white,
which made Gothic aisles of the familiar place,
while the cold struck to his thin bones
and his fingers, stinging with frost,
could hardly hold the pen.
He scrawled his name on the ice . . . Thoreau . . .
and looked forward to its melting away in spring . . .
yet spring so long in coming.
He did not solve the problem he brought here,
but he left a record of honorable striving.

Emerson respected the wild spirit
he could not comprehend.
Here is his fine old house under the urbane elms;

the warm, well-furnished library
where he wrote, or talked to friends.
Thoreau sat often by its cozy hearth
reluctant to start the long, cold walk
by night to Walden Pond.
He whittled while he listened,
thinking his own thoughts.
Emerson gathered up the slivers
when he had gone and threw them on the coals,
watching the sharp, clear flame in the azure fire:
trying to understand the fortitude
that could take a man through wind and desolate ice
back to the frail shelter of a cabin
he had built with his own hands.
Emerson sighed, and went to bed in a paneled room
grateful for the warming pan, and feather quilt,
the hot drink by the bedside,
the love by which he was surrounded:
losing, in sleep, concern for that lonely, dogged figure
trudging the road, still a mile from home.

AZALEAS

Chimney smoke trembles on gusts of wind
over the grey houses, for a century unpainted,
where the dark people live.
The stoops are rickety, not expecting visitors.

Pink and flamboyant azaleas bloom along the streets.
Deep green camellia bushes are budded in faint color.
Drowsy in the winter sun, the streets and small parks
declare the spring but the air is chill.

Nevertheless the hardy flowers will not wither.
They are a promise to the quiet people
that grace and tenderness exist,
that covenants are kept.

This city is steeped in medieval gloom at night:
ancient oaks that were here before Oglethorpe
still cast mournful shadows
in the antique light.

But in the clarity of morning one sees the dignity
of past and present where dusky children,
perennial as azaleas, gentle as pigeons,
play their timid games.

WHISTLER AT BATTERSEA

He paused just here, an evening blue as this.
In deeper blue the wooden bridge stretched high.
The swirling river strewn with clematis
drew down the drowsy sky.

Perhaps his slim hands touched this very place . . .
those shy, those eager hands that could surmise
another world, and take from off the face
of heaven, her disguise.

Before him in the gauzy tranquil air
the city seemed to hang . . . a mythic land
where stacks by day, tall campaniles were
by night, where phantoms stand

with gleaming swords that reach across the deep
of Thames, and touch the land to stars. The wise,
the pitiful, the dull hastened to sleep
and passed with blinded eyes.

Creation sang in tune to him alone.
The painter's work by poet was begun.
The web of color he would make his own
was in that moment spun.

YOUNG WIDOW

Feeding the swans beside the river,
the white determined swans,
their slender necks darting and curving
as they sail in majestic composure
over the black water, she grows less lonely.

In the garden on the upper terrace
where painted flowers lean
against the stones, and the years mourn
his absence, she listens and waits:
Slim and quiet, patiently quiet,
light in her eyes and her smile
making songs out of silence.

In the placid house with its polished floors,
its silver and Sheraton,
she is less resigned. Only where
the wide window frames the river . . .
the river like Time flowing by,
suggesting an ultimate end and a merging:
only there is she reconciled
as the stream moves away, living and restless
with its tides and its turnings,
forever escaping its sorrows, its swans.

THINKING OF SEASHELLS

I think of seashells
Scattered on long white beaches,
Glistening in the heat
Of unending summer.
Small seashells
Like hearts of china,
A pointed pink one
Perfect as a camellia petal,
Reached for through water,
A branch of coral
In the shape of a cross,
A cowry.
All in color and shape
Strangely alluring.

Once these were the homes
Of spidery
Fishlike, crawling creatures
As unrelated to their habitations
As a poet may be
To his own creations,
Or Hetty Green
To the uses of money.

As some women gather flowers,
I knew someone once,
Who loved to have shells near her:
Enthralled by intricate design,
Admiring every subtle curve,
Each delicate color,
Fingering polished surfaces
To examine texture,
Marveling how in a world apart,
Shaped by experiences
Unimaginable to her,
Surrounded by a life

Never seen out of water,
Could have come this intellectual
Beauty without a heart.

WOMAN IN GREEN

The room was a tangle of live green.
Ivy drooped from the mantel, wreathed the windows.
Chinese lilies floated stiffly on hollow stems,
myrtle adorned the pewter incense pot from the Orient.
Magnolia leaves shining as though enameled
in thick dark green, turned by halves
their pale brown sides to the mirror.
She lived among all these leaves as happily
as a shy animal secure in a wilderness,
darting here and there like a thin monkey
showing to visitors its little human tricks.

AFTERNOON IN THE THIRTIES

Vanished, the summers when we played croquet,
Driving over the rough grass through flimsy wickets.
Incongruous, the big awkward man, red-haired,
Tall, in prime of life, full of authority,
Who gambled even on this half-childish play.

Ladies in chiffon, English tweeds, costumes from France,
Shrieked in despair, as he drove some painted ball
Into the farthest hedge. Flattering eyes, lips
Admiring him, so loud, so brilliant and strong,
Beaming on all alike, encouraging romance.

His verandahed house, full of serene faces, hospitable, gay,
Welcomed arrivals in endless cars. Now vanished
    without echo,
Those famous names, sparkling words, and confident grace,
All laughing on the green with mallets swinging,
In the careless days that were sweeping a world away.

NEW HAMPSHIRE WOODS

Laced with birch,
edged with flowering laurel,
enhanced with the blue darkness
of short-needled pine . . .
a forest of fern, green moss, clear rain pools.

Through this serenity
the eye threads a quick way
into distant secrets.
The light filtering through leaves
falls upon forest flowers,
the pink lady's slipper being one.
Gentle birds invite us.

Shall we go further?
This deceptive openness
will close around us
until we are lost forever
and forsake time,
as these woods have done.
We may meet pioneers in buckskin,
from days long gone
who roam here immortal.
If we met them eye to eye
we might shrivel and disappear,
we who are not heroes,
who in times of fear
do not defend,
have strength only to escape . . .
forever asking miracles.

THE HUNGRY CHILDREN CRY

Why have we come?
There is a voice
but we are dumb.
There is a light
but we are dark.
There is warmth of love
but we are bleak,
bright raiment
but we are stark.
Alone, in fear we go
not knowing where.

THE PETRIFIED FOREST

The trees took all that the water offered.
It had come from distant places, it had soaked
through the overlapping layers of restless earth.
The trees gave back living fibres,
gave their sound and sway, their delicate groping for sun.
All that they had been, all that they might become,
was washed away, so gradually, so easily,
who can say when the day of completion arrived,
when the whole tree was impregnated,
and further change was impossible. . . .

Though they are prone
they rest upon the soil which grew them.
They are durable. They are rich and handsome,
they are heavy with jeweled wonders.
They lack only roots.

CON DOLORE

CON DOLORE

Small birds are frozen in the river.
Huddled in inadequate feathers
they are scattered upon the ice.
Unable to fly further
against descending cold,
they came down to rest upon the water.
Dark forces trapped
both birds and river in the night.
The frozen river is as helpless
as they are.
You who have wings, why should you perish?
Who seizes the pattern knows the reason.

FLOWERS FRESH FROM THE GARDEN

Violets I laid in the book
have long since crumbled:
Bits of color
brittle as wasted parchment
lie upon the page;
and I remember how once
in those last hours
when she had not spoken
for a day and a night
but had slipped beyond pain
into a strange white certitude,
she turned her head
toward the violets on her pillow.
"Lovely!" she said.
Oh, I remember
how she said, "Lovely!"
when I brought the flowers:
She, who had always praised us,
her children, who from a well of love
gave to all things praise,
turned back for an instant
from a journey already undertaken,
to speak once more with joy.

VOICE IN THE NIGHT

She ran with the wind on cold wet sands,
Stared at the sea and twisted her hands,
Stumbling blind as the light grew dim.
She listened as though the sea had spoken
Of horrors, grief, and pledges broken.
She moaned all the while a plaintive sound
That troubled the air in the eerie night,
And she sang the notes the evening long,
Yet nothing on earth was less like song.
It was the cry of a frightened child
Who wanders about with a head gone wild,
And speaks to the wind of a grievous wrong.
Who searches and mourns, as she looks around,
With a sad lost note that calls to him
Who has gone away, but she knows not where,
Nor knows where she is, if he be not there.

LANTERN

At night the Balinese boy puts
      fireflies in his blouse to light
      his way
through somber mountains.
As in my sorrow I have gathered
      all my memories of you.
Each gesture, each loving glance
      lights my way over the
      black, uneven ground
I must now cross.

THEATRE

The rain never stops.
It pounds
drop by drop
like sad, heavy footsteps
going away . . . old friends
departing, one by one.
In youth
there is a cast
of characters
and some are suddenly
scratched off the bill,
not to appear again.
So we perform
as best we can
with someone missing:
the principal role
unplayed.
Trying not to mind
on a rainy night
alone
before an audience
of strangers.

BEFORE A PAINTING BY MA YUAN

Caught in an eternal moment, they move serenely
    through time
Two sages gazing at the wonder of morning.
Aware of themselves, of spray on their faces, cloud
    and sun intermingling.
Sound of water falling without ceasing,
As words of their verses fall into the cadence
    of their mood,
As the air holds fragrance of earth, fern, pine
    and flower.
They do not see me as I stand on their terraced mountain,
Feeling the cold, cloudy mist from the waterfall,
Knowing the hidden stream below, that receives
The rushing waters in the rockbound gorge,
Listening to bird song, bright as the glittering drops
    that sprinkle
The stones of the terrace: yet I see the very texture
    of their garments,
Breathe the sweet odor of pungent pine.
The massive white stem sends out dark branches,
Throws at my feet its polished purple seeds, pagoda-shaped.
Vibrant and free, the fragile bamboo delicately waves. . . .
Is it in the wind of my arrival?
When will the teacher turn his grave glance upon me?
In what age shall I share the thoughts of his pure heart?
I shall wait here forever
Until the sage bids me approach and listen.
In this scene I have a part.

WISDOM SPEAKS

Heart, understand,
There is beauty in every land,
But a heart
Having no home to keep
Must travel light . . .
May not even by night
Reach an Inn.

KINTAMANI GUEST HOUSE

(Bali)

We were lonely, the ghosts and I.
In a swift procession of thin figures
That one could see and see through at the same time,
They blew down the mountain
Toward the dim lights of the native village.
The music of the gamelan, the shrill sound of pipes
Arose from beside the thatched roof of the temple.
It was there we had seen the dancers:
The hypnotized child, stiff as a doll,
Turning in the light of torches . . .
Walking on air.

ANEMONES

Today, my daughter, you have given me anemones:
Scarlet ones with eyes like poppies,
Dark and fringed; purples and pinks . . .
Colors so candid, so confident of beauty
That they are like a voice singing
In my quiet room: the curling green leaves
As Greek as acanthus. I remember these flowers
Spread along the roadside, as together
We made our way to the ruined temple at Eleusis
Through the Grecian rain.

MOON DOOR

I know a moon door in the Forbidden City:
In the Emperor Chien Lung's apartment this door
        is standing.
Through it I have seen pass the ghosts of an old ceremony,
Forty-eight serving men bearing the forty-eight dishes
That contained the Emperor's dinner.
But the Emperor was in love. He would touch nothing.
He sat staring at the double tree in the garden,
Thinking of the fragrant lady
Who had come but a season before from the land
        of Zungaria.
And back through the moon door I have seen them
        trooping,
Bearing the untasted food in forty-eight green
        and yellow dishes.
Silent they go, leaving him staring at the garden,
Leaving him sighing that none would dare a word
        of comfort or advice.

DARK VISION

It seemed that I was shown a scroll
That bore my name.
It taught the way to rouse the soul
In words of flame.
But I was sleeping as I read
And heeded not,
And what I comprehended
Soon forgot.

STONE

Do we at length turn to stone, all of us?
Is this the true, but concealed, end of animate creation?
Not only trees and ferns and trilobites,
But everything that breathed,
Petrified, congealed, and the living on their way,
Along with all created things, to be sifted,
Melted, changed, squeezed of essence,
Preserved?
           But this is matter only. This essence
That you speak of, this vibrating consciousness,
This link with the unknowable,
It is extracted breath by breath for other uses,

A man does not see when he is becoming stone. . . .
He hardens so little at a time.

OCTAVES

Listen for the meaning and the music
Such as razed walls of Jericho
Built Thebes, or changed the fate of Tyre.
Music that can kill upon the instant,
Freeze water, evoke fire,
Wake the slanting mind.
Music to speed growth,
Give vision to the blind,
Steady the careening stars.

Vibrating in the snake charmer's flute,
Beyond the attentive ear
Inner octaves sound.
Uncomprehending, the snake obeys,
As man obeys the singing spheres,
Not knowing that he hears.

MYSELF AND THE WATCHERS

For eons they see me struggling in the net.
When will you lie quiet, child, and learn the will
of God?

They are winged, bright, compassionate, who watch
me strain,
who see my helplessness, my useless striving
as I twist in pain,
Yet they cannot aid me, for He has bound me.
He has a use for me.

With infinite patience He waits for me to listen.
He will not speak until I listen, although
eternity continues to unfold.

It is this cord that wounds me; this gasping
in another element . . . this cold.
I try. I try to know You there. . . .

Wings move. They hear and see that Presence
hid from me.
Every leaf, every wave lifts into the mystery
of light:
But there are lesser creatures crouching near,
wingless and darkened.

O, Fisherman, make haste!

MARY KENNEDY

Mary Kennedy, poet and playwright, and the author of several books, for some years played leading roles in many Broadway successes, and a few motion pictures.

She has had seven plays produced. Two have been done in London. With her first play, "Mrs. Partridge Presents," she was co-author of a New York hit. (During its run she was playing the heroine in "In the Next Room" in a theatre just across the way.) Recently Theatre in the Street has presented two of her plays, "Ching Ling and the Magic Peach" and "Shulo." Both were played in many parts of Manhattan and environs, and "Shulo" went on to Chicago. "Ching Ling" is soon to be seen in several Scandinavian countries. Some of Miss Kennedy's fiction has been translated into German and French. Her children's books are widely read.

A traveler, she has been twice around the world, has visited many countries of Asia, has been a frequent visitor to Europe, but also knows her own country well . . . besides touring coast to coast with theatre companies, she has written stories of the less traveled areas.

She is a member of the Society of Woman Geographers, P. E. N., and other professional and poetry groups, and has become increasingly known for her poetry which appears in leading magazines and anthologies.

Miss Kennedy has been three times honored with a fellowship by the MacDowell Colony, and has won the William Rose Benét Award for Lyric Poetry given by the Saturday Review and the Poetry Society of America, and the DeWitt Lyric Award given by the Poetry Society of America, as well as other prizes. She received several citations for her volunteer work during World War II.

Her book of poems adapted from the work of Sie Thao (Hung Tu) who lived in 9th century China, "I Am a Thought of You," was published at the end of last year.

After her marriage to the late Deems Taylor, she for many years made her home in the Connecticut country, where she brought up her daughter and worked at writing and gardening.

"I think very well of these poems.

First, 'Venus and the Polar Bear' made a deep impression on me. It's a fine poem . . . the Arctic, the night sky, the confined animal, will be present to me for a long time. 'Before a Painting by Ma Yuan' . . . I can say what is said in the poem, 'in this scene I have a part.' . . . the sages, the water falling, are before me. And the Emperor who sits grieving as the forty-eight dishes of green and yellow are taken in and out, is memorable. She has a great feeling for stillnesses. The best are about stones. . . . Bede preaching to the stones, the men slowly turning . . . unnoticingly . . . into stone. . . . 'The Petrified Forest.' Then I am greatly pleased with 'Garden under Snow,' 'The Indolent Gardener,' 'Escape into Smallness.' These, to my mind, are distinctive poems.

PADRAIC COLUM

"Mary Kennedy's poems have a purity of tone and detail that make them a joy to read."

JAMES MERRILL

"Mary Kennedy's poems comprise to me all that is most illuminating in poetry. Poetry that is genuine in utterance, excellent in technique and clothed in rare beauty. Here is the work of years covering a wide range, varied and rich. Miss Kennedy is an artist, and her book is the fruit of extensive travel, close observation, life experience, and deep feeling."

LAURA BENÉT

Designed by Baron José de Vinck
Composed in De Roos twelve- and ten-point Roman
one thousand copies on Tweadweave rag-content paper
constituting the first edition